BRITAIN IN OLD PHOTO

AMERSHAM

J E A N   A R C H E R

ALAN SUTTON PUBLISHING LIMITED

Alan Sutton Publishing Limited
Phoenix Mill · Far Thrupp · Stroud
Gloucestershire · GL5 2BU

First published 1995

Cover photographs: front: Frith House, High
Street, decorated for the celebration of King
Edward VII's Coronation, 1901; it was once the
home of Hilsden's, carriers in the town, and
later Mrs Hinkley's greengrocer's shop; *back:* a
wedding group, 1913.

British Library Cataloguing in Publication Data.
A catalogue record for this book is available from
the British Library.

ISBN 0-7509-0798-3

Typeset in 9/10 Sabon.
Typesetting and origination by
Alan Sutton Publishing Limited.
Printed in Great Britain by
Ebenezer Baylis, Worcester.

The Gasworks Yard, off the Broadway, a favourite play place for children, 1890. It was
always called the Tan Yard, as a tannery operated on the right.

Contents

George Ward, (1860–1943), his wife Bessie, and his youngest son, Cornelius (Corrie). Most of the photographs in this book were taken by George Ward.

Introduction

Amersham, rich in pictorial history, had three pioneer photographers in the nineteenth century, Ebenezer King (1862–1916), Albert Haddon (1864–1936) and George Ward (1860–1943). Although the first two (both chemists) took many interesting pictures, George Ward was by far the most prolific. Most of the photographs appearing in this book were taken by him and are produced from his original glass negatives.

George was a man of many talents and his first employment on leaving school was as errand boy at King's the chemists in the Market Square. Here he met Ebenezer King, the son of the proprietor, and the two boys became friends, remaining so for the rest of their lives. King's were also printers – the first edition of the *Buckinghamshire Advertiser* was printed there. Ebenezer was already interested in photography, and it was here that George first saw the sheer magic that could emerge from a darkroom. He was hooked, and began taking pictures towards the end of the 1870s, although photography never became his main profession.

George became the manager of the local gasworks in the 1880s, living in a purpose-built house at the works. Here he built his first photographic studio, where people flocked to have their pictures taken. He married Miss Elizabeth Eagles who had left her native Malvern to become a maid at Elmodesham House. According to George's diary at the time he was fascinated by his new job and became the town lamplighter, but then he was intrigued by so many things, particularly cycles and the amazing new mode of transport – the motor car. He purchased the premises and shop opposite the Market Hall from a Mrs Rogers and, up the yard at the side (now Ward Place), he began the business of repairing cycles and cars, becoming Amersham's first motor engineer. He had three fine sons and, as they grew older, they helped in the business and sold torches, batteries and cycle parts in the small low-ceilinged shop.

George Ward also loved music. He was a brilliant violinist, travelling on his tricycle to play at chapels around the district. He formed the Amersham Sons of Temperance Brass Band in 1890 and, at that first meeting, he was elected Bandmaster, Secretary and Treasurer – and offered to teach every instrument in the band, which he did! He was fascinated by astronomy and was an accomplished ballroom dancer: some townspeople can remember his dancing very well.

Most important for the generations that came after him, and for this book, is that he was a great recorder. Whatever went on in the Amersham of his time, he was there with his camera. In his 'Index Book' he kept meticulous records of how, why, when and where he took his photographs.

The Amersham that we know today has changed a great deal from that of his day, as have most other towns and villages, in order to accommodate the ever-growing population. The Amersham of George Ward was more confined, more rural and more introvert – people did not travel far – although it had always been considered an important town. King John had granted it the right to a weekly market and September fair way back in 1201, although the Market Hall was not built until 1682 by Sir William Drake, MP, when Amersham was a borough returning two members to Parliament. The Drakes were the Lords of the Manor for some three hundred years; they lived at Shardeloes, the house visible from the Missenden Road.

John Knox (the Scottish Reformer) had considered it a town of sufficient consequence to make it his last stop on 16 July 1553 while on a preaching tour of Buckinghamshire in favour of Lady Jane Grey. In the seventeenth century the people of Amersham grew accustomed to daily musters of Parliamentary troops passing through on their way to Aylesbury, and it is said that Oliver Cromwell himself dropped off for a meal at The Griffin. It is a pity that photography and George Ward were not yet in existence to record these chequered highlights of Amersham history.

He was around, however, to photograph the coming of the Metropolitan Line to Amersham Common up on the hill in 1892 and the building of the station in 1894. This created the new town of Amersham on the Hill, and George photographed its beginnings. He was there to capture the atmosphere of the Amersham of the First World War, and to portray all the varied facets of the town – the industries, the shops, the fairs, the farms, the schools and, perhaps most important, the characters. The result is a glimpse of a way of life that has faded into history.

Amersham bathed in sunlight, 1885. The view is from Ruccles field looking across the valley to Shardeloes.

Section One

THE TOWN

*Amersham in 1890. This photograph, taken from Coleshill Fields (the site of today's
bypass) shows the smoking brewery chimney, the rectory on the hill to the right and a
Windsor chair factory to the left.*

An aerial view of the old town, 1923–4. The new council estate of Piggott's Orchard is in the process of being built. The small white building seen in the Broadway at the end of Dovecotes Meadow housed the fire brigade's horsedrawn fire cart.

Aerial photograph showing the town hall (now called Market Hall) and the position of the Alley (between the Market Square and the Broadway), which was demolished under a slum clearance order in 1939 (see p. 12). The Memorial Gardens now stand partially on this site.

Amersham on the Hill in the 1920s, showing Oakfield Corner in the foreground and the vacant site of Woodside Close on the right, which was not built until 1930. Sycamore Road is devoid of shops, which appeared some time later.

Amersham on the Hill during the 1960s, showing the railway, Hill Avenue leading to Oakfield Corner in the north, and Sycamore Road branching off to the right. Woodside Close – now developed – can be seen clearly with its central green.

An early film entitled *As He Was Born* was made in Amersham in the early part of the twentieth century. Some locals worked as extras and this plaster statue prop was erected in the Market Square.

The bottom of Whielden Street, as seen through the Market Hall arch, 1884. In the background, the cottages forming the Alley culminated in the Market Square.

Under the Market Hall, 1884. The arch on the right was blocked up as a result of the Public Safety Act of 1911 which required that public buildings should have two exits. A second flight of stairs was built in its place.

Looking towards the foot of Whielden Street and the Market Hall from the Broadway in the 1890s. Note the shoes hanging outside the shoe shop on the left; part of the Alley complex is on the right.

The Broadway showing the Alley, 1884. The Alley was the centrepiece of the town and comprised two ancient rows of cottages with a cobbled way through. The Broadway end culminated in the quaint building at the centre, Mrs Dobson's cottage. The Alley was demolished in 1939 under a slum clearance order despite protestations from the residents and townspeople.

The narrow, cobbled way of the Alley.

A wider view of the Broadway, showing the Alley and electricity sub-station, *c.* 1930. The Griffin public house is on the left.

Market Square, with cottages of the Alley complex on the left. The Crown public house is in the foreground.

Market Square and Market Hall at the turn of the century. The manager of Clark's Stores on the right (now the Foodhall) is reviewing the situation after a particularly bad storm.

The High Street facing east. The Red Lion public house is on the left.

The drawing room of Elmodesham House when the Cheese family of solicitors was resident there in 1883. Originally called Woodville House, it was renamed by the Amersham Rural District Council at the time of their purchase in the 1930s.

The dining room at Elmodesham House, 1883. Some of the murals that came to light on the sale of the house in 1986 are visible.

The High Street looking east, at the end of the nineteenth century.

Once a medieval farmhouse, the first of these cottages in the High Street has sixteenth-century murals of the Nine Worthies adorning the walls. The development at the side is now called The Worthies.

The wide part of the High Street facing west, which was always called The Crescent. This photograph shows the house known as Whiteposts, because of the two white posts that stood outside for the tethering of carriage horses.

The top of the High Street with the bottom of Cherry Lane on the left and Turpins Row on the right.

A gentleman of Amersham in his conservatory at the turn of the century.

The rear garden of The Firs (now known as Piers Place), 1895, when it was the home of Dr Potts. It remained a doctor's home or surgery for Drs Gardner, Johns, Rolt and Davidson.

The Missenden Road. The photograph was taken just past the little white lodges near the entrance to Shardeloes Drive where the River Misbourne crossed the road.

The entrance to Pipers Wood, nineteenth century. At the top of this road through the wood there was once a small hamlet called Pipers.

Wilkins Meadow, *c.* 1900. This meadow belonged to Mr Wilkins, the coal merchant, until the Brazil boys purchased it as a site for their first factory in 1929 (see p. 53). Over the following years this factory gave employment to a great proportion of Amersham people until it was sold in the 1960s to Bowyers. Now it is the site of the mighty Tesco.

Bury End, the London end of the town. The old waterworks is on the left. The cottages on the right were demolished in the late 1940s.

Bury Farm, where William Penn (1644–1718) courted his first wife, Guilelma Springett. She was the stepdaughter of Quaker Isaac Pennington, who lived here with his wife Mary. Another prominent visitor to Bury Farm was Thomas Ellwood (1639–1713), who was engaged as tutor to the Pennington sons.

Bury Farm with the wall of Dovecotes Meadow on the left and Gore Hill, the road to Beaconsfield, on the right.

The London end of the Broadway. The cottage on the left bears a notice warning all 'Common Beggars, Ballad Singers and other vagrants' that they will be apprehended and dealt with according to the law.

Women gathering next to the little shop at the entrance to Norwoods Yard. James Norwood was a well-known trader in the town at the turn of the nineteenth century.

George Ward's shop, opposite the Market Hall, at the beginning of this century. Here he sold cycle parts, torches and batteries, etc. The shop was recently known as Heddon's.

Whielden Street before the turn of the century, with Bright's shoe shop on the right.

Whielden Street in 1890, with Crown Farm on the right and the Windsor chair factory on the left.

Scott's the butcher's, 1895. The meat hangs on display while the Scott family poses for George Ward. Their descendants still live in Amersham.

The laying of the gas main in Whielden Street, 1910.

The Union/Workhouse gates in Whielden Street, 1895. Whielden Street became known for a while as Union Street.

The glorious new Amersham Workhouse, 1895. Built in 1838 to a design by Gilbert Scott, only four years after the passing of the Poor Law Amendment Act, it later became Amersham General Hospital.

The Infirmary, built in 1905, which later became the maternity wing of the hospital. It is now the Hebden Centre.

The Queen's Head public house nestling in the hollow of the hills in Whielden Lane (the upper part of Whielden Street).

The Queen's Head public house in Whielden Lane, 1890. Until the sale of the Weller Brewery in Amersham in 1929 the Queen's Head was a Weller pub, one of the 142 licensed premises owned by them within a radius of 35 miles of Amersham.

The foot of Whielden Street, 1885. George Ward has deliberately positioned these people for the photograph.

St Mary's Church photographed while under restoration in the 1880s, when it was clad in split flints. The church dates from the thirteenth century.

St Mary's Church in the early twentieth century, looking smart after its restoration.

The interior of St Mary's Church in 1895, with polished pews and candelabra lighting.

Amersham Choirs Festival, 1934. The popular rector Charles Briggs is in the centre of the first standing row.

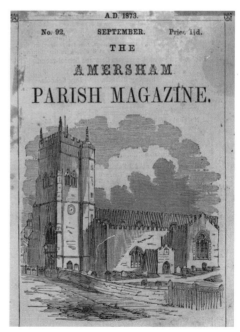

The *Amersham Parish Magazine* of 1873, the year St Mary's School was built.

Miss Watson's Sunday School class, 1936. Among the pupils are Hazel Darlington, Barbara and Margaret Wright, Muriel Carter, Betty Robinson, Iris and David Woodbridge (now in Tasmania), Tony Wright and Gladys Rance.

Verger George Longland at the door of St Mary's Church, holding a loaf depicting the loaves and fishes, 1953.

Miss Mabel J. Cornabé, a pillar of St Mary's Church, Sunday School teacher and founder-leader of the Girls' Club. She was also the first woman to be elected to Amersham Parish Council, in 1934.

The Baptist chapel, in a photograph taken by George Ward at the turn of the century. Built in 1784, it is reached via a footpath from the High Street.

The Baptist chapel where the footpath carries on up to the Platt, showing the graveyard at the rear, 1890.

Mount Zion, the upper Baptist chapel, in the Platt which runs down into Whielden Street, 1884. It is now a private house.

The Methodist church, built in 1899. It is the youngest building in the High Street.

AMERSHAM
ON THE HILL

Building the station, 1894. The Metropolitan Railway line came to Amersham in 1892,

forging its way across the hill above the old town, after which Amersham on the Hill

mushroomed into being.

Station Road, *c.* 1900. The road was improved to serve the station; later houses appeared on either side.

Nazing Cottage, near the top of the hill and backing on to Rectory Wood. It was once the home of Mr Williams, the builder.

The top of Station Road near the railway bridge. There is a small parade of shops on the left, and on the other side a draper's, later known as Renshaws.

The International Stores in the same small parade of shops, at the turn of the century. It abutted on to a building that once served as a cinema, and later as the famous Playhouse Repertory Theatre; it is now the Auction Rooms.

The Station Hotel (right; now known as The Iron Horse), 1894. On the other side of the road is the Temperance Hotel (now the offices of Amersham Town Council).

Oakfield Corner in the 1920s. More modern shops were being built in Sycamore Road and Hill Avenue.

Sycamore Road in the early 1930s, showing a private house and the new Regent Cinema.

The Free Church, Sycamore Road. Built in 1913, it has now been rebuilt on Sycamore Corner.

White Lion Road on Amersham Common, 1915. The road was probably straightened when the common was enclosed in 1815. The sign of The Pineapple public house can be seen on the left.

Drayman Jesse Gomm delivering Weller's beer to the Boot and Slipper in Rickmansworth Road, 1899.

SHARDELOES

The swans that were resident on Shardeloes Lake

for many years, a source of beauty and pride to the

people of Amersham. This photograph was taken

by Ken Slade in 1936.

Shardeloes House in the eighteenth century. It was built in the 1760s by Stiff Leadbetter, although Robert Adam had a hand in the interior decorative work. The parkland was designed by Sir Humphrey Repton.

Shardeloes House and lake, photographed by George Ward in 1915.

Local lads Eric Rance, Jess Freeman and Ken Slade at Shardeloes Lake, *c.* 1932.

Shardeloes stables with grooms, 1929. 'Tich' Alder is second from the right.

Mrs Drake (the Squire's wife) on her favourite hunter at Shardeloes, 1890.

The Old Berkeley hounds in their kennels at Coldmoreham, 1914.

A 'smart turn out at Shardeloes' (George Ward's description), 1895. There are two horses in this brake outside the stables.

George Knowles, *c.* 1930. He was the landlord of the Hare and Hounds (now demolished) in Whielden Street; he lived and breathed horses, and taught the Drake children to ride.

Shardeloes Lake, *c.* 1910. The lake regularly froze over in the winter and gave great enjoyment to the townsfolk for skating and sliding. Just to walk across to the island in the middle was an epic adventure (below).

Section Four

THE SHOPS

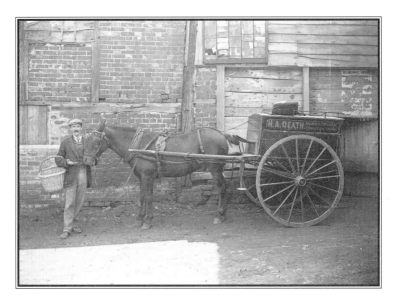

Mr Death standing in his yard with his horse and van, 1890. He had his baker's premises in Whielden Street.

Mead's grocer's, *c*. 1880, showing the bottom of Whielden Street. By the turn of the century new wide shop windows had been inserted (below) and Mr Mead stands proudly at the door. It is now a hairdressing salon.

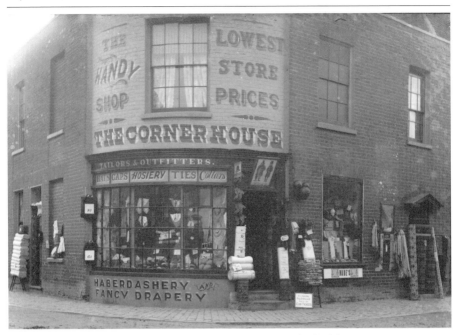

The Corner House clothes shop (Wade's) on the corner of Whielden Street, 1890. It was owned at that time by Ernest King, brother of printer Ebenezer King.

The small shop window shown above. Vests, shirts and bowler hats with price tags are clearly visible.

The toy shop of Mrs Aldridge in the High Street, facing the bottom of Cherry Lane, 1889.

Fuller's draper's in Whielden Street (often called The Emporium). The shop was high ceilinged, with chairs placed at regular intervals along the lengthy counters, and the service from Mr Fuller and his assistants was impeccable. It is now an antiques shop.

Mr Arthur Steven's butcher's shop, 1904. It was tucked away behind the Market Hall in what is now Market Walk. Here Mr Stevens stands with a prize bull and some assistants.

Mr Stevens, a side of beef with a huge amount of suet, and Mr W. Pusey, who later had his own butcher's shop adjoining The Griffin.

Bailey's antiques shop near the top of the High Street at election time. The Baileys were also cabinet makers.

Town Mill when the Royal Bucks Laundry collected and delivered.

John Brazil, one of the family who began a successful sausage, pies and cold meats business. He was very fond of horses: here he is at a point-to-point.

An early Brazil van taken outside the factory by Peter Hansford. Commissionaire Mr Auger stands by.

Ebenezer King (1862–1916), who took
over the family business from his father,
Thomas Howes King. The Kings were
printers and chemists for many years (see
the Introduction).

On the death of
Ebenezer in 1916,
his wife Jane took
over, passing the
business over to her
son, Thomas
Rowland, as soon
as he was qualified.
Here he stands in
the shop in the
1960s with his
popular wife, Elsie.

Mrs Jane King with her three daughters and two cousins, 1901. This photograph was taken by Ebenezer King at the rear of his premises.

The post office in the High Street. Today it is situated further down the street, but it can be seen that this is how Post Office Yard became so named.

Postmistress Miss Bettesworth in 1915, after she had retired to live in Post Office Yard. Her father was Postmaster before her.

Section Five

FARMING

Turkey plucking and trussing at Brickwick,
Christmas 1896. Brickwick was at the end of the
footpath from Amersham to Coleshill.

Haymaking in Rectory Meadow, 1915.

Women working in Wych Field (at the back of the school) before the turn of the century.

Haymaking at Bury Farm, 1899.

Ernest Matthews showing off his prize cow at Mantles Green Farm, 1912.

Mr Butler holding the horse for Mr Howells at Coldmoreham, 1910.

Drake Ayres, a local tramp, *c*. 1911.

Pondwicks, in a photograph taken from the River Misbourne in 1924 by Hilda Chilton.

Pondwicks, looking towards the river and the back of the High Street, 1910.

The Whit Monday cattle fair in the Market Square, 1902. The cottages in the centre were part of the Alley complex demolished in 1939.

The cattle fair in the Broadway outside The Griffin, 1885.

The Amersham Horticultural Association, founded in 1934, grew some fair-sized onions. (Photo: Gordon Davey)

And their marrows weren't bad either! (Photo: Gordon Davey)

Whit Monday cattle fair, 1890. The photograph was taken from George Ward's bedroom window.

Section Six

THE BREWERY AND
MALTINGS

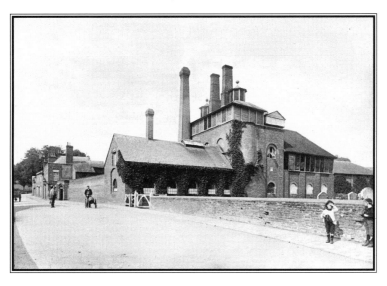

The Weller family took over the Brewery in Church Street in the eighteenth century and eventually employed nearly half the male population of the town. All the Weller estates were sold off in 1929.

The rear of the Brewery building, 1889.

Brewery workers wending their way home in Church Street, *c*. 1890.

The Maltings in Barn Meadow, built by the Weller family in 1829.

Some of the workers at the Brewery pausing for a photograph, among them 'Bobbin' Cox and Mr Redrup, *c.* 1913.

The Brewery forecourt showing the barrels of beer, 1888. Goya International later purchased these premises and employed many townspeople.

Clem Ford, manager of the Brewery, c. 1908. He was a keen sportsman: here he displays some of his trophies.

The Ford family complete with goat cart, in Barn Meadow at the rear of their property in the High Street.

The Brewery float in the Broadway, taking part in a parade to celebrate King George V's Coronation in 1911. Note the draymen in their red-tasselled hats, white overalls and sacking aprons.

Drayman Banning on his dray in Station Road, *c.* 1900.

Drayman Freddie Gomm delivering Weller's beer somewhere 'up the line'.

The King's Arms in 1915; it was renovated in the 1930s. The first film on highwayman Dick Turpin was filmed here, with Ronald Coleman playing the lead.

The Nag's Head in Whielden Street when part of it was a baker's shop, *c.* 1900.

The Swan at the top of the High Street before the turn of the century. The cottages just before the entrance to Cherry Lane were demolished shortly afterwards and replaced by the terraced houses there today.

Popular landlord Bert Tooth leans on the bar of the Swan, *c.* 1951.

The Chequers at the London end of the town, *c.* 1900.

Weller's family coach outside the Chequers, 1883.

Tom Gilbert, whose uncle kept the Chequers at the beginning of the century, enjoys a pint in the garden.

The Red Lion in the High Street, *c.* 1890. The premises next door comprised a butcher's shop.

PEACE AND WAR

Mr Wingrove, the town crier. This is George Ward's
picture of an even older picture (1860s or 1870s) which
was still in its frame when he took it.

The Boxing Day Meet, 1906. The photograph was taken from George Ward's bedroom window.

The same Meet in the 1950s when John Brazil, as Master of the Old Berkeley Hunt, led it past The Swan.

A Boxing Day Meet in the Broadway in the 1930s.

A fine horse at Coldmoreham, 1918.

The Lower Baptist Sunday School outing outside the King's Arms, setting off for Burnham Beeches, 1890.

The outing has reached the Market Square.

The happy band progressing up Gore Hill. The horse had his hat on for the occasion.

The arrival at Burnham Beeches. All that was there in those days were the grotesquely shaped beeches and donkey rides – not forgetting the picnic!

The splendid wedding reception when Miss Elizabeth Gilbert of Amersham married Mr Herbert Slade of Coleshill, 1913. The reception was held at the Wheatsheaf (now demolished), which stood opposite Bury Farm.

A photograph from the wedding of George Longland to Lena Hale, the daughter of the verger, c. 1930. On the retirement of Mr Hale, George filled the post himself, remaining verger for many years. In this photograph Llewellyn Baker supports George whilst Lena Randall is bridesmaid on the right.

Right: A dancing bear in the High Street, 1880. The street rapidly cleared of people when the dancing bears went through. *Below*: All the dogs disappeared as well, until the bear had gone, when 'the scent brought them out in droves', as George Ward records.

The fair in the High Street, *c*. 1890. In 1201 King John granted to Amersham by charter the right to hold a weekly market and a September fair. The market is now held at Amersham on the Hill, but the fair still comes to the old town every 19–20 September.

The fair from the bottom of George Ward's yard.

The 'big roundabout' in its usual place in the wide part of the High Street, 1930.

The fair in the Broadway, 1924.

Fair day, 1894. In that part of the street narrowed by the Alley, opposite the Griffin, the hot-chestnut lady is ready to ply her trade.

The fair, 1974. This picture was taken from the roof of Elmodesham House.

The Oddfellows Fête and Flower Show, Amersham's biggest day, which was held on a Thursday (early closing day) in August. The opening parade started at Town Mill and traversed the length of the town to enter Dovecotes meadow (otherwise known as Duffats).

The Fête in 1900. George Ward has captured the sheer excitement of the day, as the Amersham Band leads the parade with the Oddfellows' banner held high. Note the children clad in their finery.

All sorts of fun taking place in the meadow, 1910. Shows, competitions and races were held, together with a small fair brought by the Beech family, the aristocrats of the show world.

AMERSHAM SPORTS. 1911
START FOR "MARATHON RACE".

The Amersham Marathon, the highlight of the day. This is the start in 1911 (after the event had moved to Rectory Meadow). The winner was the hero of the town for the following year.

A popular event at the Flower Show – the pillow fight on a pole. Ebenezer King, in trilby, looks on, while Dr Henderson and an adversary try their skill.

Not the Flower Show but a small gathering which took place in the field fronting Rogers Wood, above Bury Meadows.

Jack o' the Green, a country pastime taking place in the Broadway, 1882. Dressed in greenery, the people played musical instruments and collected for charity. The two figures in the foreground must be on their way to Bury Farm for milk.

A celebration of some kind outside the Crown with Dilly and Dally, possibly during the First World War.

The King's Royal Rifles gathering in the Broadway, waiting for the Squire's agent to inform them of the address of their billet, 1914. During the First World War, the Kings Royal Rifles were billeted in Amersham, Missenden and Chesham.

The King's Royal Rifles drilling in Pondwicks. They were inspected by King George V in the High Street in November 1914.

Wartime atmosphere captured in the High Street. The girls on the right (outside Haddon's, the chemist's) are definitely giving the eye to the soldiers striding down the comparatively traffic-free street.

Bayonet practice outside the Brewery.

Officers and gentlemen posing at the rear of Elmodesham House, 1915.

'Stumpy' Garton, Headmaster of St Mary's School, looking good in his uniform.

Lady collecting for a bullet for the Kaiser. His frightening face appears on the replica.

Land Army girls in the First World War: Cis Wright (Lippeart), Nancy Jarvis and Kate Wright (Hurst).

Local lad Jack Archer, who joined up at the age of sixteen in 1915, having lied about his age on the advice of the recruiting sergeant.

Young Mary Gilbert and Cis Wright, who longed to help the war effort, could not resist dressing up in uniform. With no Womens' Army available, they cooked for the Royal Flying Corps at Watford.

The Armistice service of 1918, held in the parish church.

The memorial cross to the Amersham boys who did not return from the war was installed in the churchyard in 1919. It now stands in the Memorial Gardens.

Many a heart was breaking at the ceremony, including that of Mr 'Bobbin' Cox who lost both his sons.

SPORTS AND
ENTERTAINMENT

Will be given in the

TO WN HALL . . . .

. . . . **AMERSHAM.**

(By kind permission of T. W. T. DRAKE, ESQ.)

ON THURSDAY, NOVEMBER, 30th, 1899.

ADMISSION:—Reserved Seats 2s. Second Seats 1s.

Tickets and Programmes may be obtained of MR. KING, CHEMIST
where a plan of the Hall may be seen.

DOORS OPEN AT 7 O'CLOCK. CONCERT TO COMMENCE AT 7.30.
Carriages may be ordered for 10.15.

KING, PRINTER, AMERSHAM.

Promotion for a Grand Concert in the town hall on

30 November 1899, to be given by the Amersham

Fire Brigade.

The Horse Racing Committee, 1894. The Squire stands out in the middle of the back row. To the right of the back row (with the beard) stands Albert Haddon, and Will Wright (foreman of the Maltings). In the second row, sitting on the left is Clem Ford and the three brothers Weller, owners of the Brewery. At the end of that row is Mr Dumbarton the butcher. Ebenezer King is fourth from the left in the front row.

The Amersham cricket team, *c.* 1920. The Captain, Revd C.E. Briggs, is sitting in the centre of the front row; among the players are Harry Atkins, Joe Hoare and Hugh and Tom Orton.

Shardeloes Estate cricket team, 1930. Harry Wright, Arthur Slade and Jack Archer are in the back row, second, third and fourth from left; Mr Wilkinson, the umpire, is on the extreme right. In the second row (from left) are W. Day, estate foreman, Herbie Slade, the Squire ('Teddy' Drake) with his dog, and Major Wilson, estate manager. Wilfred Kelly is in the centre of the front row.

The Amersham Town football team in Barn Meadow, 1896, dressed up for some occasion. The team was started in 1890 by the Revd E.B. Cooper (Headmaster at Dr Challoner's School). Mr Cooper is in the centre of the back row, with high hat and beard.

The team c. 1910. Included here are 'Porky' Palmer, C. Line, Jim Redding and Horace Freeman.

The team in 1923/4, having won the High Wycombe Challenge Cup. Among them are Jack Archer, Laurie Haddon, two brothers Martin, Jack Sealey, 'Stumpy' Garton, Horace Freeman, E. Carter and Dick Lane.

The team, again in the 1920s, after a successful season.

The team yet again. Spot the familiar faces.

The Boxing Club in 1934, proudly displaying a considerable number of cups. It was formed in 1930 with Lord Chesham as President. Among those pictured are: Gomm, Stonnell, A.J.L. Ferguson, Dr Gardner, Dr Johns, two brothers Stone, Grace, Edgar, Watson, Claude Taylor and R. Atkins.

The swimming pool in the River Misbourne at Dovecotes, built by community-minded Chris Newton after the Second World War. The children thoroughly enjoyed it, but unfortunately it was closed by the Health Department.

Two decorous ladies posing with cycles and dog, 1905. Cycling was a popular pastime at the turn of the century.

The Amersham Sons of Temperance Brass Band, 1890. It was formed by George Ward, who was elected Bandmaster, Secretary and Treasurer at the first meeting. This photograph of the Band is taken in that first year: the bearded George stands on the left.

The band in smart new uniforms, 1892, when it had broken away from the Sons of Temperance. Here 'Dibe' Keen is on the big drum, Tom Baker (standing, left) is on the trombone and Jim Redding is second from left, front row. George Ward (Bandmaster) is the bearded figure in the middle.

The Band at Chenies in the 1930s. Herb Fountain has taken over as Bandmaster. Among these smiling lads are two Saunders brothers, G. Revel, T. Dover and Les Keen.

The Band in later years. It fell away during the two world wars owing to loss of manpower, but started up again in 1977. Among those pictured are their conductor of that time, Nigel Tolliday, Les Keen, Len Stratfull, Gilbert Bryant, Derek Gwynne, Sid Morris, Bill Lovell, Rod Stevens and Roger Speller.

A show in the Market Hall, then the town hall, 1888. The Fire Brigade were very fond of producing such shows.

Mary Gilbert dressed ready for her performance in a local production of *The Mikado*. The photograph was taken at Holmwood Terrace, 1913.

SOUVENIR PROGRAMME

of the first

HOME GUARD

BALL

held at

BADMINTON COURT
OLD AMERSHAM
BUCKS

Friday, March 5th

from 8 p.m. to 1 a.m.

by 11th Bucks Batt Home Guard

Organised by the Battalion Entertainment Committee
with co-operation from Battalion Ladies' Committee

LUCKY
NUMBER

304

1/-

Years later a Home Guard Ball was held at Badminton Court in Church Street.

Edward VII's Coronation celebrations up on the hill in the village of Coleshill, 1901. Mr Stubbings, headmaster of the school and an artist of great repute, is supervising.

A concert party ready to perform at the Union/Workhouse, *c.* 1912.

Amersham British Legion Women's Section choir, 1930. Conductor Mrs Stone is at the centre. Among those gathered around her are nurses Dixon and Young, and Mesdames Keedle, Johns, Revel, Archer, King, Tompkins, three Mason sisters and Miss Fuller. They 'dashed away with a smoothing iron' to their heart's content.

Amersham (Old Town) Women's Institute in their 1975 production of *Jack and the Beanstalk*. From left to right: Doris Merrell, Joan Wherry, Eileen Kuhles, Sylvia Stevens and Julie Clarke.

SCHOOLS AND SCOUTS

Amersham St Mary's School, 1910.

Amersham Infants II, 1906. Tom King in a large white collar sits in the front row.

Amersham Girls' Group I with teacher, Miss Godden, standing on the right. Pictured here are, among others, R. Kaley, R. Scott (Thornton), K. Wright (Hurst), M. Gilbert, E. Keen (Cater), Hilda Chilton, L. Hale (Longland), H. Scott (Wilson) and Aggie Dobson.

'Mr North and his class', 1890. George Ward's note is all that is known of this group.

Boys' Group II, obviously 'Stumpy' Garton's class, *c.* 1897.

Mrs Edith B. Kelly standing with her class, *c.* 1919. Mrs Kelly came to Amersham St Mary's in 1918, and became Headmistress of the Girls' School. An outstanding teacher, she stayed until 1943.

The Amersham Baby Clinic, which was held at the British Legion Hall in Whielden Street, *c.* 1934. The names of some of the families represented here are: Maynard, Hazel, Darvill, Hegarty, Kaley, Taylor, Bizley, Revel, Wright, Sawyer, Rix, Johns, Ayres, Edwards, Witney and Woodbridge.

A London Transport children's tea party held in the Market Hall in the 1950s.

Mrs Monzani's Dancing School, 1970. This excellent school has operated in the Community Centre for many years.

The Amersham Scout Group in 1912, with Rector C.E. Briggs in the centre, Horace Freeman on his left and Tom King in the front row on the left.

Horace Freeman (1889–1980). He was a keen scoutmaster and stalwart of the Amersham Town Football Club, supporting and working for them in various capacities from 1908 until he died. He was also a well-known referee.

Section Ten

PEOPLE

Mr Ayres, the blacksmith, 1886.

Mr Redrup enjoying his pipe, 1888. His descendants still live in the town.

Mr J. Hazel, the gamekeeper who lived at Cowpastures, 1888. Note that the dog's lead is hitched to his belt to leave his hands free to shoot.

Cis Wright and Mary Gilbert in a pretty pose at Green Gates, 29 High Street, 1912.

Mother and daughter, 1892. George Ward has not recorded the names of these two ladies.

The members and officers of Amersham Rural District Council in 1943, a photograph taken at the hospital. Centre front is Alfred Woodley (Chairman); back row, second and third from left, are H.E. Buxton, Clerk, and Jean Cutler, Committee Clerk.

Amersham Town Council in 1978, when Councillor Leslie Mackay was Mayor, Keith Halifax was his Deputy and Peter Ridout was Town Clerk.

The opening of the Community Centre in Chiltern Avenue, showing (left to right) Molly Tench, Secretary; Cllr Rex King; Major Boyce, Chairman of Amersham RDC; -?-; and Ronald Bell, MP.

The staff of Tudor & Co., 1943. Tudor & Co., a firm of Lloyds Insurance Brokers and one of many city firms evacuated to Amersham during the war, occupied The Gables, Hervines Road.

Francis and How, the oldest firm of solicitors in the area, 1966. Here the staff line up at the rear of their offices in the High Street to mark the retirement of Mr Howell Davies (centre front).

The typists at Goya International pausing for a break in 1949; from left to right, Jean Archer, Pat Gomm, Molly Pitcher, Joan Sabatine, Nancy Caudery, Daphne Haddock (Pratt) and Pam Appleby. Goya International had their factory and offices at the old Brewery buildings (Badminton Court) in Church Street.

Dr John Rolt, who came to Amersham as a young man in the 1930s. He rapidly became a favourite of the people.

Dr Johns, who lived and practised from The Firs in the High Street. He played an active part in the community life of Amersham.

Dr Helen Davidson. Amersham reeled when this popular doctor was murdered in Hodgemoor Wood in November 1966 while walking her dog. So far as is known no one has ever been charged.

The local constabulary, *c.* 1920. The building in the background appears to be the Maltings in Barn Meadow.

Young Fred Clifton, who came from the Grenadier Guards to become a police constable at Amersham. Being on the reserve, he was called up immediately war broke out in 1939. Happily he returned to the local police after the war ended.

The first accident in Amersham High Street. How on earth did it happen?

Cottages at Coleshill, which were destroyed after a very bad fire in January 1914.

The Chief of the Amersham horse-drawn fire brigade, 1890.

A fireman of the same time resplendent in his helmet.

'The Malt House after the fire last night, 1884' (George Ward's note). It is now a hairdresser's.

Self-portrait by George Ward
later in his life.

The young Mrs Georgina Gilbert, 1880.

'Old Mrs Sears of Coleshill', as George Ward recorded, not very flatteringly.

'Mrs Toovey's little girl', in George's studio, 1889.

An unknown young woman.

Mr Randall (butler) from
Coleshill House, with Annie
Swarbrick (maid), in drag, in
George Ward's studio, 1895.

Mrs Higham-Hunt from Hyde Heath posing outside Apsley House and the King's
Arms, 1902.

Acknowledgements

To George Ward, above all. Other photographs in this book are from family albums and by unknown photographers, and I would acknowledge with grateful thanks those people who have loaned them: Mrs Grace Taylor, whose husband Claude was an early member of the Boxing Club; Daisy Clifton, whose husband Fred was a member of the local constabulary; Betty Dallemore, a descendant of the King family; Dot Morris and Gerry Dyche of the Knowles family; Mary Baker, whose knowledge was invaluable; Peter Hansford, Pam Joiner and Meg Green, who helped in so many ways; and last but not least Duncan Russell, who skilfully produced such excellent prints from George Ward's original glass negatives. There are still enough to fill another book.

'Wickliffe Preachers', and the children gathered around them, at the turn of the century. Strange to think that other Wycliffe preachers came to Amersham in the sixteenth century, which resulted in Lollard burnings up on Ruccles Field.

BRITAIN IN OLD PHOTOGRAPHS

To order any of these titles please telephone Littlehampton Book Services on 01903 721596